you still have yourself

you still have yourself

fernando samalot

PRIMERO
SUEÑO PRESS

ATRIA

New York Amsterdam/Antwerp London
Toronto Sydney/Melbourne New Delhi

PRIMERO
SUEÑO PRESS

ATRIA

An Imprint of Simon & Schuster, LLC
1230 Avenue of the Americas
New York, NY 10020

The authorized representative in the EEA is Simon & Schuster Nederland B.V., Herculesplein 96, 3584 AA Utrecht, Netherlands. info@simonandschuster.nl

First Primero Sueño Press/Atria Paperback edition October 2026

PRIMERO SUEÑO PRESS / ATRIA PAPERBACK and colophon are registered trademarks of Simon & Schuster, LLC

Manufactured in the United States of America

1 3 5 7 9 10 8 6 4 2

The Library of Congress Cataloging-in-Publication Data has been applied for.

ISBN 978-1-6680-8936-1 (pbk)
ISBN 978-1-6680-8937-8 (ebook)

For my daughter
Mar de Luz

I thought I knew
love

I thought I knew
joy

I thought I knew
purpose

I thought I knew
life

but then you came along
little one

and the day you were born

so was I

even if all you have left
is yourself

that is still

a whole universe
you have.

PREFACE

Remember Me as a Time of Day

The year before my daughter was born, I joined a fathers' circle to prepare myself for the man I was about to become. At the end of one of the sessions, the facilitator asked a simple question:

If you had to describe where you are in your life right now as a time of day, what would it be?

A specific image quickly appeared in my mind:

A soft rain at golden hour, just as the morning sun is rising.

That has always been my favorite weather phenomenon. The marriage of light and water makes the veil feel thin between what has been and what is about to begin.

One week later, my daughter was born in the early morning.

It rained softly as the sun rose
and the light of my life was born.

That image and concept stayed with me and eventually became the way I wanted to present this book.

You Still Have Yourself is divided into five sections, each embodying a time of day, each held by a different part of me that has guided me through cycles of self-discovery, loss, and return.

First Light is the Story, a timeline of how this book came to be.

Golden Hour is the Lover, the part of me that feels enchanted by life, beauty, connection, awe, and presence.

The Long Night is the Melancholic, the one who descends into grief, shadow, and isolation, and grapples with the deep work that happens when no one is watching.

A New Dawn is the Sage, who acquires quiet wisdom and emerges when experience turns into understanding, and suffering softens into meaning.

Evening Star is the Elder; this section is a reflection about my life set fifty years in the future.

That's the scope of what you hold in your hands right now.

This book is my witness. A chronicle and testament to all my former selves who had to die and become soil for me to grow into who I am now. A collaboration across time between who I was, who I am, and who I am becoming.

My intention with this book is that it serves to accompany you in the way it's accompanied me, through whatever season you are in. Whether you are basking in the golden hour of the peaks of your life, traversing a long dark night of the soul, or finally awakening to a new dawn, may this book serve as a companion and reminder that every season has a reason and that everything that has ever happened to you was only ever meant to bring you closer to yourself.

prologue : first light

All of my most beautiful beginnings started with an ending.

What do you have left after losing everything you know? Everything you've built your life around? Your home, your relationships, your career, your community, your health, your identity, and your sense of belonging?

I once wrote these questions down on a crumpled piece of paper and slid it across the table to my first true love, who by then had found the love of her life elsewhere but whose wisdom I still trusted. She held the pen so softly in her hand as she wrote her answer, smoothed out the edges of my torn page, and passed it back to me.

You still have yourself, she wrote.

It was the simplest answer to a burning question I had ever received, even if I couldn't fully grasp it at the time.

That was twenty years ago, but her words would go on to accompany me through countless seasons of life, loss, death, and rebirth.

Some of those seasons would one day become the book you are holding right now.

The first began in 2017, when the most disastrous storm of my lifetime tore through my home island of Puerto Rico and completely uprooted the life I had known for thirty-two years.

In the wake of that storm, I lost my home, my community, my long-term relationship, and the connection to nature I had built my entire artistic identity and sense of self around.

What followed were some of the darkest nights of my life, quite literally. The house I was now living alone in wouldn't regain electricity for months. In those long nights, I was forced to come face-to-face with an inner darkness I had spent years avoiding. Many nights I felt haunted by my own shortcomings, my mistakes, and my flaws of character. I felt trapped in my hopelessness until I reached my lowest point, the very edge of despair.

It was there, when all hope seemed lost, that I was thrown a lifeline. A gift that would change the trajectory of my life and open my world to endless possibilities.

The gift came in the shape of a camera, a tool that would allow me to spend the next two years traveling the world alone as a wandering artist and poet.

Many of the poems in this book were born during that time.

Being alone with myself, so far from the home I knew and free from any preconceived notions of who I had to be, taught me how to belong inwardly.

Witnessing how I showed up in an unknown world with a fearless, open heart completely transformed my relationship to myself.

It was the first time in my life I truly felt that I loved who I was becoming.

Then life shifted once again.

At the end of that long journey, I returned home to Puerto Rico in 2019 and entered a relationship that would go on to shape one of the most formative, accelerated, expansive, and challenging chapters of my life.

I remember reading somewhere once that if you want to evolve at an accelerated rate or gain unparalleled wisdom, you should either get married, have a child, or develop a serious illness.

Life, in all its tragically comedic genius, decided to offer me all three in rapid succession, within the span of two years.

Each of these transformational milestones asked many things of me. They asked me to surrender parts of myself and to dissolve identities I had spent my whole life nurturing.

In the process, an old, familiar pattern of mine resurfaced. Mistaking self-abandonment for devotion, I began surrendering parts of myself no one had even asked me to give up. I stopped writing. I stopped creating art. I stopped tending to the parts of me that made me feel alive, believing that doing so would protect the peace I was trying to build.

Parts of that surrender shaped me into the man and father I am today, and for that I will forever be grateful. Other parts, however, hardened into deep wounds and resentment that eventually made my body shut down on me, forcing me to spend the worst part of three years living with a neurological illness no one could name or explain.

In the search for answers, my small family of three relocated to New York City in 2022. I arrived there broken, disoriented, and unsure who I was beyond my pain and responsibility.

What I didn't expect was how deeply that city would hold me.

New York didn't give me answers for my condition, but it gave me distance from old wounds and permission to rebuild myself as an artist, a man, and a human being again. In the busiest city in the world, I found community, I found expansion, I found presence, and I found a version of myself I thought I had lost.

For the three years we were living there, I built a life as a full-time artist, traveled the world—held up by a cane—to exhibit my artwork, and decided that I wanted to finally publish my first book of poetry and writing from that long-gone season of my former travels.

I remember thinking, *I don't think I'll ever write another book, but at least I can immortalize that past version of me from when I was at the peak of my life.* Even as I was building a new world for myself, I continued to romanticize my former selves, a recurring habit of mine. I believed that if any part of me deserved to be preserved, it was the young, wild, free, connected, and healthy version. There was no place, in my original vision of this book, for the ill, married, frustrated full-time parent I had become.

It was from that place this book was first imagined.

I worked on the manuscript for months, intending to quietly self-publish the book. I saw it as a closing gesture, a way of gathering the poems from my years of travel and offering them as they were, without expectation.

It was my wife who encouraged me to think differently. She believed the work deserved a wider life and that I could reach for more than I was allowing myself to imagine.

So I decided to pursue a publishing deal, with what I assumed was my already completed manuscript.

When this deal finally came through, when my dream publisher expressed interest in my work, it felt both affirming and ironic. I had just accepted the idea that I wouldn't write again, only to find out that life had other plans for me.

We love the book and we want it, the publisher said.

It just needs to be twice as long.

Well, isn't this poetic? I had to write a whole other book.

Almost immediately after signing the book deal, my life began to unravel once more.

In a sudden turn of events I never anticipated, our family had to move back to Puerto Rico, a place that hadn't felt like home in a long time.

What I returned to was not the island I had left years before, but an isolating shoreline filled with old wounds and unresolved grief. Leaving New York had stripped me of the community it had taken me so long to find, and the momentum I had built for my art career came to a sudden halt. Then, only two months after returning, despite our best efforts to hold back the rising tide, the foundation of my marriage finally gave way, and my wife and I chose to let the ocean claim what was left of it and allow our relationship to transform into a conscious and respectful co-parenting partnership.

In many ways, I found myself in a familiar place, similar to where I had been in 2017. Only this time, the loss was much more profound.

The move, the separation, the grief, and the task of rebuilding my life on my own for the first time in seven years created a deep paralysis within me. I couldn't write. Not a single line. I watched deadline after deadline pass, asked for extension after extension, unsure if I would be able to finish what I started.

What I didn't understand yet was that this season of not writing wasn't a failure. It was my final initiation.

It took me so long to finish the book because I still had to live its final chapter before I could complete it.

It wasn't that I was writing this book. *This book was writing me.*

On Father's Day of 2025, after five months of still living together with my daughter and her mother and navigating our new dynamic, I finally moved alone into a small studio apartment tucked away in a forest in the town where I grew up.

That first night, something in me finally gave way.

Like a river that had run dry for years but was suddenly revived by a torrential downpour, the words began to flow through me again.

And once they started, they didn't stop.

Day after day. Night after night. Everything poured out: the grief, the relief, the release, the remembering. I realized then that the version of me I had once believed was unworthy of being in this book was precisely the one the book had been waiting for. Who *I* had been waiting for.

Not the man who traveled the world.
Not the man who got sick and lost himself.

But the man still standing here now.
Writing these words.

Present. Broken open. Alive.

Finally able to let myself be exactly where I am, inside the chaos, the depth, the beauty, and the truth of this moment.

So when I ask, What is it I have left after having lost everything?

I have everyone I've ever been,
every part of me I've ever loved, lost, and recovered.

I still have myself.

golden hour

The Lover

There are several key instances in my life that shaped my understanding of what love means to me.

In the version of love that I learned as a kid, movies, books, and other works of fiction all sold me on the idea that love was this uncontrollable, intensely dramatic, overwhelming, and almost fatalistic emotion that had the potential to both elevate me to the highest heavens or sink me into the deepest hells.

For as long as I can remember, especially in my childhood, I had always been a hopeless romantic, and this version of love—built around infatuation, desire, craving, and attachment—made all the sense in the world to me.

So I fell for it.

All the way in.

Early on, through cycles of recurring themes and repeated patterns, rejected love letters and torn-up poems, I realized that I came to this world to learn what love is by experiencing almost every version of what love isn't.

Some would say that this overly sensitive kid with the world's most open heart never stood a chance, but I beg to differ.

Behind every pain and heartbreak, there was always a new depth of love that revealed itself to me.

Unrequited love taught me to love unconditionally. That my love was mine to give and that love in itself was a gift, regardless of whether it was returned or not.

Jealousy taught me that belonging isn't ownership. That I'd much rather be wrapped in flowers than in chains.

Betrayal and Infidelity taught me the importance of radical honesty, open communication, and building trust based on maskless Truth.

Attachment and codependency taught me the importance of boundaries and of staying true to myself.

Control and dominance taught me that devotion is inspired, not demanded, and that the truest love I could ever give was the feeling of freedom. Freedom to be, to feel, to choose, and to be chosen.

All these lessons that I learned, almost way too early on, were focused on an external manifestation of the love that was always inside me. I was meant to first experience versions of love in relation to others before I could turn my gaze inward and finally arrive where I was meant to.

My golden hour.

The moment where I would connect with the ephemeral and ever-changing love of Nature.

Whatever pieces were still missing, in my quest to understand love, I finally found by immersing myself in the natural world and allowing myself to learn from it.

Have you ever witnessed a fleeting moment so beautiful that it feels as if time has stopped? A moment you wish could last forever? Like floating in an ocean of bioluminescence under the Milky Way; or watching the sun shine across the valley surrounded by mountains, where you finally felt at home; or falling asleep on moist soil in a forest full of fireflies; or waking up to a soft rain falling on a golden morning, on the day your first child is born.

All these moments hold a kind of love and beauty that I never had words for before, but that I finally learned to appreciate. It's the beauty of impermanence.

Impermanence taught me that the love I was always looking for isn't only in other people. It has always been all around me: in the cold mountain air that caresses my skin, the warm Caribbean tide that crossed whole oceans just to lie at my feet, the first ray of light that shines on dewdrops, and the slow, rising fog that exhales off the earth.

Love was never finite. It wasn't transactional. It could never be lost or wasted. For this love, it is enough to simply be witnessed. Like a flower you admire but don't need to pick.

This love is a way of seeing.
A way of being.

A love made of awe.
A love made of awareness.
A love made of sublime and embodied Presence.

Whatever version of love is alive for you right now—romantic, devotional, unrequited, unconditional, familial, natural, or simply present—I hope you will receive all the visions of love that exist in these pages and connect with the one that you need the most.

May you find yourself living in your own golden hour.

I'll offer you a trade,
she said.

Everything for everything.

I didn't get it at the time
but Life,
oh,
she had plans for me.

Go live
and grow
and write,
she said.

The story spoken
across the valley of your soul.

And so
I have.

And so
I am.

The world has grown
much bigger since then.

I can feel my heart has too.

I can feel my heart.

Love is real. It is vast and limitless. It's not something meant to be measured or put in a jar on the top shelf for safekeeping. For how could you fit the ocean into a cup? You simply cannot. It's as vast as it's meant to be free. It flows, grows, and glows in the spaces between us, and the more we love, unconditionally, selflessly, unattached, and without fear, the more beautifully our love blossoms.

Fear not, mi amor, true love does not fade. It is a state of being that we attain by loving more and more and more and more.

So try this, corazón: Fear less, love more, and we will find ourselves somewhere along the way.

I need you to remember this:

Regardless of who you've been
or what you've done,

you are still worthy of Life
worthy of Joy
worthy of Forgiveness
worthy of Compassion
worthy of Support
worthy of Understanding
worthy of Unconditional Love.

You are worthy.

So please
let yourself receive.
Let yourself be seen.
Let yourself be loved.

Loved like you deserve.

Loved—
like I've loved you forever.

My dearest,

I do not need to
see you
hold you
keep you
or own you

to love you

how could I ever
ask the wind
to stay still for me?

I only want to love you
like a gentle breeze

to caress your skin
to play with your hair

to fill my lungs with thoughts of you
and exhale you back into the air

so that anywhere the wind takes you
anywhere your heart takes flight
you will forever find my love for you

always present
always willing
always light

I want to know the hidden parts
of the garden of your heart.

Not just the flowers blossoming.
Those are the easiest to love.

Show me your thorns
and withered leaves.

I want to water all you are made of.

Could you pause here for a moment?
could you listen openheartedly?
without a hook or a catch?
without me having to ask?

after all,
I'm sharing this for you
but mostly
it's for me

the speed at which these years go by
has turned attention into a commodity
and I honestly don't think that kind of speed actually works for me

I don't want to rush the seasons
or try to match anyone's pace
I mean
sharing my honest truth was the reason
I started doing this in the first place

so I want to do just that
make my whole life a single long, perpetual, selfless act
an unbridled and unconditional
honest and luminescent
expression of my own

sublime
embodied
presence

every year
the springtime
bursts and blooms

time
and time
again

regardless
of how harsh
a winter

trust me

you can too

we can too

Ay
mi amor

this light you see
and love in me

it's all inside you too

I am only
your reflection
shining back at you

If all I ever have with you
is this one fleeting moment
then even more
I'll want to love you

before you float away

Let it come up to the surface

wherever pain lives in your body
whatever ache sleeps in your heart

let the light that shines between us
reach the deepest, darkest parts

and let it come up to the surface
so it can finally be met

not with fear
not with resentment
not with betrayal
not with regret

but only with love,
amor

Only in Love

Love needs space to grow.

A sacred space
A nurturing warmth
A caressing light
A comforting sound
A calming presence
A forgiving embrace.

Love needs grace

and so do we.

So do we.

I may not know you
but I love you just for being here.

Loving yourself is also
letting yourself be loved.

It's surrounding yourself
with people who see you,
the real you,
and treasure you
in all your honest, vulnerable,
messy, chaotic, and beautiful glory.

Knowing your infinite worth,
which was bestowed upon you
when you first came into being,
means you never settle for less than that.

If any of my words ever resonate with you, it's because they're inside you too. We are all here as messengers to remind each other of our deepest truths. Whether unknowingly or intentionally, we're always channeling for each other. Exactly what we need to hear to heal.

In this way,
I learn from you and then try to be better.

In the same way,
you learn with me and then we grow together.

If that makes us sound profoundly connected,
it's because we are. It's because you are.

I'm just here to remind you.

in case
you cannot find it
anywhere else
today

here it is

a gift of
unconditional love

you don't have to earn it
or even give it back

just receive it
if you need it

and know that you deserve it

you always have

can I stay here in this moment?
can I keep this single one?

when my memory is long gone
can I come back here

and just

keep chasing this spring sunset
forever with you?

can I keep this single one?

no matter how apart from me
you're forever a part of me

you don't have to chase after me,
she said.

just go wherever the light takes you
and I will meet you
somewhere along
the way.

Across most of my relationships growing up, I always tended to be a very attached person. I'd tie my identity and sense of safety to others and push my ideas of "forever" on them.

This approach, of course, was bound to create suffering and was destined to fail, as the reality of people as well as nature is that everything is forever changing.

Life is movement, it's an inhale and exhale, it's ephemeral and temporary, and therein lies its true beauty.

Once I let go of the idea that things had to last to have real meaning, I opened my heart and life to a whole new level of emotional depth and connection.

Life became about witnessing, experiencing, and appreciating things and people as they were, in the moment they were in front of me.

The same way I cherished the wind in my hair or the waves that traveled across the ocean just to caress my feet for a moment, I learned how to love as an act of presence.

The truest and most liberating form of love I've ever known.

It was always easy for me
finding beauty in your softness

my golden guiding light

so I knew growth had come
when in the harsh midday sun

I witnessed you
and stood in awe

when life shows us its beauty
I will stand in awe with you

when life feels scary or uncertain
we can brave the storm
together

whenever life is hard
we can face it all head-on

and whenever life is sad
I'll be your refuge forever

in this and every lifetime

wherever we may be

more than all the light in the sky
and all the water in the sea

my heart is in your heart

and the part of me that lives in you
will always love
the part of you that lives in me

Love and Light met once in a forest
and from their union you came to be

then, from the sweetest dream
upon waking

you came to me
you came to me

life can be this weightless

to just lie upon the grass
after a soft rain has passed

and let the breeze carry your longing
across the valley of the wind

true intimacy lives
underneath all the layers
and masks we wear
between ourselves

if you want to bridge
the great divide
that separates
your heart from mine

show me
show me

show me your real side

You were silent for so long
I was sure you had forgotten me,
but as the wind picked up
and all my memories of you
rose up over the mountaintops,
I could've sworn I heard your voice again.

After all this time,
it's still my favorite sound.

Love will happen upon you
like a soft morning rain.

she is a roaring river
and a burning phoenix
bursting with life at the seams

if you cannot become
a proper vessel
to hold her
build upon her
fan her flames

then you have to let her be

let me be

I want to be the wind
that fans the flame
inside your heart

my dear

here I am
thinking I know you
and once again

you surprise me

yes

there are
hidden worlds
in you

still left for me to discover

I left a gift
for you

tucked away
in the first time
your shining eyes
met mine

you might
not remember
me
as I was back then

but
I'll never forget

even after all that's left of me
is but a faded memory

my love lives on forever

beating softly
in your chest

I let myself forget again
for a moment
why they chose me

a thousand times
I've lost my way
and every time
out of the darkness

your guiding light

she shows me

The seeds you sowed in me,
I have nurtured them with love.

Now,
after years of devotion,

the seeds have finally sprung.

don't ever let
the world convince you
that softness equals weakness

fields of light
grow beneath your feet
when you walk
with grace and vulnerability

I'm not waiting for tomorrow.
I'm not counting on forever.

I want to feel love,
give love,
be love,

here and now.

So even if again
all of this slips through my fingers,
I know that I won't have any regrets.

No excuses, no doubts,
no longing, no craving.

I was who I was.
I gave what I gave.
I was present and grateful
every step of the way.

I can ask for no happier ending than that.

all my pasts and futures
beating softly in your chest

carried by the wind
somewhere only you can feel them

I'll be your reflection

so you can see yourself how I see you,
so you can love yourself how I love you.

surround yourself
with those
who can love
the way you love
and witness
how your world
suddenly lights up

My love journeyed across oceans
just to lie upon your shore.

I was never looking for an easy love. An up-in-the-clouds, head-over-heels, ungrounded kind of love. An unrealistic, bound-to-be-disappointing kind of love.

I'd been there and done that before, a few hundred times over.

What I wanted, in my silence and aloneness, was a willing kind of love. Willing to show up. Willing to be raw. Willing to face and embrace both the darkness and the light. Willing to own what's theirs and grow from it.

A love that was willing to do the work.

So years from now, when I catch myself looking back at the invisible path I paved for myself and observe the happiness and peace I created, I'll have the satisfaction of knowing that it wasn't just a gift from the gods or a serendipitous alignment of the stars, but the result of the energy I have willingly put in.

Reminds me of something my father once told me that will stay with me forever.

On a day that felt like the end, he said, "On the easy days I am grateful. On the not-so-easy days, of which there have been many, I am grateful. Why?

"Because I know I am exactly where I chose to be."

Back in the beginning, in the closeness of our embrace, she looked into my eyes and said, "I'll keep you wild, and you keep me safe."

It was one of the first promises we ever made to each other.

Of course, we had no way of knowing at the time—that what we were offering each other would inevitably become what we'd be tested on the most.

Life has a funny and almost twisted way of delivering our lessons to us.

Healing isn't always pretty. Hell, it almost never is. Not until you're on the other side of it. It can really be the most excruciating and challenging thing you will ever do—and that's just by yourself. Doing it with others adds a whole universe of depth and complexities. Some days you may find yourself questioning everything you've done. Every choice you've made. Every step you've taken. Sometimes it can break apart everything you thought you knew about yourself.

If it's so challenging, then, why stay? Why rough it out?

I can only speak for myself, of course, but all my life, my most difficult and heartbreaking tests have been followed by the most transformational and heart-opening moments of growth and expansion.

I've always known this.

That's why I've always chosen to keep moving forward.

Because in my heart of heart, I've always known that at the other side of the stormiest of seas lies a brand-new world, waiting for us. A world where we can finally be

wild
and safe

and free.

The work we do on ourselves is not only for us. The whole of humanity benefits from the love we become. When we heal our wounds, that love resonates back through our roots to also heal our ancestral suffering. When we heal, all our pasts and futures heal as well. I'm trying to heal not just for myself, but for all of us and those who come after. I want to leave something of real value behind when I finally cross over.

I want the world to inherit my love.

everywhere I've ever been
and everyone I've ever loved

has become a part of me

I remember the feeling of closeness
of being held
of being loved

I remember simply being

I remember how you felt
how you looked
how you smelled
as I pressed my ear against your chest
and heard that familiar beating

It was the sound of home

I remember getting closer to you
close enough to feel your breath on me

It was in that closeness
that I saw you shine
like a ray of light from the midday sun
piercing through the forest
and whispering—

thank you
and goodbye

me despedí del sol

"you let me leave
and I'll let you go"

our final act of love

the long night

The Melancholic

I used to be afraid of the dark before I understood that was where my light was born.

Like the seed that has to break through layers and layers of soil before it can bask in the light of the sun as a flower, or the caterpillar that completely dissolves itself in its chrysalis in order to become a butterfly. One thing is clear: It's not in running away from it but in surrendering and embracing that darkness by which the deepest transformations take place.

This has been true for me as well.

So much of the light I've imbued this book with has come from some of the longest, darkest nights of my life. Ones that I wouldn't have survived if it wasn't for the Melancholic, a version of me who has been with me for as long as I've been able to feel and express emotion.

The same sensitivity and openheartedness in me that gave birth to the Lover would, when faced with pain, heartbreak, rejection, or humiliation, collapse and bury themselves in the deepest, darkest parts of me. They laid their roots down in those depths of isolation, where for years they remained, feeling unseen, unheard, and unworthy.

Growing up, it was this part of me that I struggled with the most, and I spent a lot of my formative years learning how to take care of it.

In one particular season in my twenties, while I lived in a farming commune with some friends, working with the earth would once again bring me one of my deepest life lessons. It taught me that when nurturing and caring for a garden, you can't simply trim weeds at the surface level and expect the work to be done. Real growth will ask you to get down on your knees, sink your hands deep into the dirt, find the root, twist, lift, and unearth what is unseen but felt. Then every single thing you pull out, every wilted version of who you used to be, will eventually become part of the soil from which a new life will grow.

I came to understand that my sadness was never a hindrance to my growth, but an essential nutrient in my garden of becoming. Its roots would stretch across my entire life and intertwine to form a map of who I've been, who I am, and all the parts of me that still need my love.

In the end, that's all my sadness ever asked of me: to care for it with compassion, to listen with patience, and to nurture it with grace.

The Long Night is my invitation to dive into the depths of our melancholy and discover what hidden truths the dark wants to reveal to us.

Come, dive in with me.

Please,
be soft with me.

I am worn
from holding strong
so long.

Everything feels
like it's the first and last time lately

like I'm saying goodbye
just as I'm arriving

like tomorrow isn't guaranteed
and this moment is all I have

but by the time I realize it

it's already gone

Afraid, ashamed, small, weak, alone, misunderstood, anxious, unsafe, trapped, invisible, irrelevant, redundant, insignificant, abandoned, betrayed, replaced, ridiculed, rejected, exiled, silenced, forgotten . . .

As hard as it is
and as much as it weighs,

I must keep reminding myself

I am more than what my pain tells me I am.

I am the salt of the earth
poured on reopened wounds.

The jagged mountain peaks
that make and break my bones.

The cold winter wind
and the soft cloth against your skin
that was never enough
to keep you warm.

I am everything I've always been
and nothing as you see me.

Please,
return me to the silence,
where my solitude is sacred
and I can finally remember
how pain, like all things,
is only temporary.

This moment,
like everything,

is only temporary.

I know it can be exhausting.

All these heavy thoughts we carry around. So many expectations, disappointments, regrets, and ideas of what could or should have been. Oh, my dear. The day you decide to focus that energy back on yourself, you are bound to realize: There's no need to carry that weight around. No need to throw your back out.

Promise me this. Next time you find yourself lost in those thoughts, just remember to breathe. Breathe in this present moment.

Just be here. With me. In this moment.

Where only love can live.

I don't want to let my dreams
slip through my fingers
just because I was afraid
of letting go

even as I lay here
withered and forgotten

seeing her
in all her splendor
made me remember

I, too, can someday blossom
again

Please,
dear light,

don't let
my reminiscing
keep me from
your loving presence.

I only want to be
here and now.

A pattern I have noticed:

Regardless of how well I'm doing, I always tend to look back and romanticize my past selves.

Thinking back to when I was younger, healthier, fitter; was more well known; had more friends or less responsibilities—it always feels as if moving forward comes at the cost of parts of me I love.

This, of course, is a mental trap. A behavioral pattern I repeat when I feel unhappy with where I am.

The useful thing about mental traps is you can train yourself to get out of them and, in doing so, transform them into powerful tools for growth.

If you work on yourself with patience and compassion—that's to say, the patience to repeat the same mistake a thousand times and the compassion to give yourself grace, love, and encouragement through it—then waiting for you on the other side of that struggle will be a lighter, healthier, happier, and more satisfied and liberated version of yourself.

It's a lifetime of work, and commitment is everything.

That's why I have to keep reminding myself of this.

Whenever I catch myself drifting from the present moment, I repeat it a few thousand times more.

I only want to be here and now.

I only want to be here and now.

I only want to be here and now.

Here and Now.

I am.

I know you will find a way

I've gotten way too comfortable in my sadness. Even knowing well no one has ever changed the world from their comfort zone.

I don't have that high an ambition, though.

I just wanna change myself.

Prove to my inner me I can pull myself out of it.

Just watch me,
tangled-up heart of mine.

Watch me begin again.

Even if there is a chance
things might not get better,

still
I have to try.

I can't keep waiting
to find myself again.

For the spark to come back.
For the love to flow again.

I have to unearth
from within me
a new way of being.

Become a new kind of water.

Here
in this chaos
in this darkness
in this uncertainty,

only here and now
can I become someone new.

New.

Again.

For the first time.

However fearsome the world can be,
I am safe in here

with me.

Perhaps
the answer I am hoping for
will come floating to me
on the back of the rising tide

then again

maybe it won't

I am learning
to make my peace
with both

I lost sight of her
somewhere along the way.

The softness in my heart
I promised I would keep safe,

yet in the silence of my defeat,
buried underneath my shame,

I swear I could hear
the faintest whisper say,

"It's okay . . .
Love is still a choice
we get to make each day."

So
at least I have that.

I still have today.

At night I open portals
to the depths of my longing

down
to its withered roots
I dive

to tend to them with the care
only I can give

where have I been all this time?
and who is this living in my body?

down
past the layers of my aching
I dive

to the truth in my memory
only I can know

how far back does this story go?

past the shame in my bones
and my need to be seen

dive down
to the source
that's been calling to me

to forgive
to return

to the love that I am
to the love that I know

only I can be

I've spent
far too long
scouring the depths.

Please,
let me catch my breath
before you pull me
back in again.

If I'm being honest
I can't really say
I love myself,

at least as I am now.

But believe me,
I am trying,

trying to remember
the way that it felt—

Self-Love's warm embrace around me.

How she spoke and how she held me
lingers somewhere in my memory,
and even though I've lost sight of her now
and forgotten in my sadness,

if I still myself for long enough
I know she will return to me.

My love
always returns to me.

How many times
have I had to start over by now?

Feels like anytime I get used to
a new version of myself,
life comes rushing in to remind me:

Don't settle.

Don't trap yourself in stories
or in all that could've been.

There is always something new
waiting for you
just around the corner.

Don't settle.
Don't trap yourself.

I'm here.

We've got this.

I hope
someday you feel
brave enough again
to share
the parts of yourself
the world forced you
to hide away

your love deserves
to be felt and witnessed

If I ever let you
get this close,
it's because I chose
to trust you.

To bridge chasms in our whispers
and break patterns in our confidence.

Our eyes became a mirror
to reveal our own unconsciousness

and so we grew into each other
in the closeness of our hearts,

ever changing,
ever flowing,

once together,

now apart.

I'm grateful
you planted a forest

I know that we dreamt of tomorrow

but

I wanted to lie in your shade

not wither away in your shadow

There are places we will see
and people we will be

only once

cherish it

I wouldn't ask you to stay.
I already knew from the start:

You came to me
to be the wind
that fanned the flame
inside my heart,

so now that my soul is burning
and the longest longing gone,
I can finally release you
and let you carry on.

My love of loves,

carry on.

Nothing is out of reach
if you're willing to go the distance

As long as we have breath,
we can start again.

I can see you trying.

I can see you.

I know growth can be hard
but it's important to remember:
It doesn't have to be
only hard
all of the time.

It's okay to take a break.
It's okay to ask for space.

We're in this for the long run.

It's okay to catch your breath.
To grow at your own pace.

I can see you trying.

I can see you.

I'll be here,
in the space between dreams.

In the lingering scent
of your memory.

In the moment you choose
to come home to yourself,

I'll be here.

I'll be here.

be patient with yourself

the seed in your heart
has to break through
layers and layers of darkness
before it can become a flower

but it will

you will

I still believe in you

I've been slowly peeling back the layers
off years of self-abandonment
and wondering at what point
it became so hard for me
to trust myself

I mean

I say I wonder
but I know

I did this to myself

trapped myself in a story
even though I know full well
we become the ones we tell ourselves the most

so why did I let ghosts
be the ones to write mine for me?

as if my future could belong
to a past that doesn't know me

anymore
not anymore

you don't know me anymore
but I'll count that as a blessing

'cause one thing I know
about my life

is all of my worst stories
always hold my greatest lessons

how long was I asleep?

it feels like a whole lifetime
has come and gone

I woke up with a sour taste
lingering in my mouth

this must be the "forever"
I kept hearing about

I made it out of bed
but I barely recognize this place

and try as I might
I can't wash these years off my face

now the only thing left for me is
surrender

and to start my life over again

so it seems

at least I can say
with a sigh of relief

I'm done living in somebody else's dream

I have to admit
I'm not there yet
but at least I can say
that I'm on my way.

Don't falter,
my heart.

The ocean will calm
and your moment will come.

Let's just let the waves crash
for today.

All that's left of you
is a feeling on my skin.

Now it's mine to give.

Now I'm mine to give.

To all the moments
that nearly broke me:

I'm not putting this on you.

Even if you hurt me,
it's not on you to heal me.

Who I am and choose to be
is my decision and mine alone.

I am no longer the victim
of anybody's love or lack thereof.

I understand that sometimes
we come into our lives
to be catalysts for change
and you were
the perfect storm I needed
so I'd never be the same.

I'm not doing this for you
or for anybody else.

Forgiving you is a gift I am giving myself.

Your memory's a necklace
that weighed heavy on my chest
but I finally remembered
what you whispered to me
in the deepest part of my silence.

Piercing through the void,
it was your voice
that came to me and said,

"Forgiveness is Liberation,
Gratitude is Transformation."

I thought I had misplaced this lesson
somewhere between worlds
but I unclenched my palm
and there you were,
as close to me as you had always been.

I looked upon you for a moment
and saw lifetimes
of what had been and never would be
stitched together like the quilt
that kept me warm as a child.

I wrapped myself with you
and remembered fondly how it felt
but in my heart I knew
that it was time.

So I held you close,
closer than ever before,
close enough you could hear me faintly whisper—

I love you.
I forgive you.
I thank you for the lessons.

And I let you go.

The answer's been in front of you all along
but unless you change your focus
you're never gonna see it

I'll remind you once again
my wounded inner child of habit

for as many times as you need

just because you've done something forever
doesn't mean you have to do it forever

the longer I wait
to come back

the harder it gets to remember

what is it about
this silent weight I am carrying
that's so hard for me to surrender?

I thought I'd know better
since I've been here before

that this pain isn't healing itself

but I've spent all this time
feeling sorry for me

when I should've forgiven myself

for the longest time
we wandered
lost
deep in the thick of it
but I think
now
since surrendering

it's all beginning to feel lighter

hold on to yourself
corazón

even the longest night will not last forever

it can be lighter

we can be

In every corner of your heart
you find fear—
plant a seed.

Tend to it with love
and one day you will walk
through your mountain of flowers,

wild in your blooming
and finally free.

everything is moving
so fast
too fast

and
all that I can do
is try
to slow down

all
the
way
down

until all that is left
is this one
present
moment

I am safe here

years of untold stories
etched upon my skin

a plea
a prayer
an offering

to find my place
to be safe in my body
to feel at home

to finally return

to me

“no one is coming
to save you”

I know

but

I am someone

aren’t I?

and along
the path
back to myself

I will never leave your side again

It's taken all I have
to show up as I am now
but the more that I surrender
the more it becomes clear

I won't let myself forget

I am more than just the patterns
in someone else's broken mirror

I wrote you
a thousand letters

each one in
a different language

I thought at least
in one of them
you'd finally understand

me

all
I
ever
wanted
was
to
be
known
by
you

without
the
need
to
translate

everything
I
am

Suddenly,
an opening.

You are closer than you think.

You always have been.

All I ever yearned for
turned out to be my greatest lesson

to learn to love without losing who I am
and to let myself truly be without losing what I love

She still lives inside of you.

She does.

Even if you've lost sight of her now.
Even if you've lost touch.

Her strength,
her love,
her passion.

Her wisdom,
her compassion.

Her joy.
Her confidence,
her power.

It's all still inside of you.

She
is still inside of you.

Forever holding you close.

The version of yourself
you loved being the most.

Fear not
dear child of light

your love is not lost

it's like the burning sun awakening
and piercing through the morning fog

forever rising in the east
and setting in your chest

like a deep inhalation that fills you
only to release again

out unto the world
and into every open space

into the mountains
the valleys
the forests
the lakes

hear them sing for you
in gratitude
for the gift of every breath

songs that awaken your memory
should you ever forget

they say

"fear not, dear child of light
for even if you cannot see us now

your love
your heart
your hope
your dreams

we never really left"

at night I lull myself to sleep
and whisper songs of thankful longings

I never knew
my grief and gratitude
could harmonize this calming

There's a future version of you
looking back at this very moment
with only love and compassion.

Don't take yourself for granted.

You are already
on your way.

I came back
but I'm not here yet.

You caught me in a really weird time in my life. A transitional period six years in the making. I'm back on my island, although it hasn't really felt like I belong here yet. My family moved away and I don't really know who my friends are anymore. I'd been feeling lost and lonely, so I did the only thing that made sense to me—I immersed myself in nature. The same in which I first found myself, many lifetimes ago. These waters know me better than anyone. They hold my tears and carry my secrets. They cleanse my mind and my weary body when nothing else can.

Today, for the first time in a long time, my loneliness became aloneness again and in those cold rainforest waters I finally felt like . . .

I'm home.

I am (not) alone in this.
Trusting myself
also means
learning to trust in others.

all that time I spent waiting
for the right moment to arrive

the right moment to live
the right moment to be

as if such a thing
could ever exist
anywhere outside of me

and yet
still I waited

held back
hid away

sat alone in my storm
while my life washed away

I did try
holding on
but I knew I couldn't keep her

I thought I'd survive the flood
but I only ever sank deeper

deeper
and deeper

until
I hit the bottom

and suddenly all became still

"will you trust
and surrender
to this moment,
mi alma?"

I have

I am

I will

I'm loosening
my grip.

Surrendering
to what's coming.

Letting myself
grow with the flow.

I can't wait to lie
with the version of me
that finally dared to let go.

It's all coming apart
and falling together
in the most beautiful, chaotic way.

Everything is.

Even though my role's been recast
and my mask turned to ashes,

I somehow feel like I can
breathe again.

Even though it was not up to me
how the end of this story unfolded,

it brought the pain in my body
up to the surface

so that I could finally hold it.

I can trust that it was meant
to be this way

since the trembling in my hands
subsided

and my truth was always
meant to be shared

even if my shame
begged me to hide it

so I'll let my life tell my story for me

all the things that I failed at
but tried
and

even though I can't say
what tomorrow will bring

I can choose what language I'll write in

How long has it been since you last sat and connected with yourself? I mean your truest self. Your deepest, most secret self. The real you that's hidden underneath the layers of pain, anger, and shame you've allowed to weigh you down—to hold you back. I only ask because I feel you, and I feel you because I am you.

It's been too long.

I know the way back home feels long and winding and you're exhausted, but if there's one thing I have learned, it's that the only way back is moving forward.

Inward and onward.

So I am taking the first step. Again. One I've taken countless times before and one life will have me take forever more.

I am listening, again. Deeper, truer, even more honest. For the voice that's always whispered the longings of my soul.

I am trusting, ever fearful as I am. Even as my knees feel heavy and shaky. Even as my body feels like caving into my chest. I am trusting in the strength that lives within me and allowing it to lift me, hold me, speak to me.

I can hear you. I can feel you. I believe you.

Guide me home.

For all the times
you dimmed your light
so others could feel comfortable

you can forgive yourself

for not knowing in that moment
how empathy without boundaries
could harm you

you can forgive yourself

for walking away
from your soul's secret garden
to go tend to someone else's

you can forgive yourself

for taking so long to realize
and now having to crawl back to you

you can forgive yourself

I can forgive myself

I forgive myself

to anyone who ever hurt me
I forgive you

to everyone I ever hurt
I am sorry

all is forgiven

a new dawn

The Sage

If every single horrible thing that's ever happened to me has brought me to this moment, then I can find it in myself to give thanks for it.

Not because I romanticize suffering, but because now I understand that every wound, every heartbreak, every dark night of the soul I've ever overcome, has slowly, over decades, carved out a path for me to become who I've always felt I was born to be.

This learning started to become clear when I noticed how so many of my painful experiences and hardships seemed to rhyme with each other. The recurring themes, characters, and patterns of my life lessons have been so hyper-specific to my own personal development that they feel as if they were written solely for the purpose of my growth.

Once I understood that—that life wasn't happening *to* me but *for* me—I could finally surrender to my journey, fully trusting that none of it is in vain, that none of it is wasted, and that even the hardest challenges are only meant to bring me closer to my highest self.

No number of spiritual teachers, guides, coaches, ceremonies, or scriptures could ever teach me what being fully present in my own life and my experiences could.

Who could ever understand my own story better than the one who lived it?

What else could contain the lessons I came to this world to learn?

My life *is* my holy book.

If the Melancholic is the part of me that dives into the depths of my darkness to unearth what is hidden there, then the Sage is the one who brings him back up to the light so together they can turn that experience into lived wisdom.

The Sage is the one who has learned to see with eyes unclouded, who has heard harmony in the chaos, found the lesson in the wound, and cleared a path from the pain to the purpose.

A New Dawn is the embodiment of that. It's the quiet understanding after going through the storm. It's the exhale of surrender and the soft relief of trust.

As you traverse this last section, dear reader, I invite you to ask yourself:

What wisdom has your pain gifted you?
What are the recurring themes that shaped it?
What hidden truths are you remembering?
What awaits you at the edge of this new dawn?

life offered me a precious gift
and held it gently for the world to see

it was all the love I'd ever given
returned a thousand times to me

there's a season for everything

a season of storms
a season of rest
a season to sow
a season to harvest

same way
there's a reason for everything

a reason to keep going
a reason to push through
a reason to start over
a reason to choose you

every season
has a reason

this is just the one we're in

none of them will last forever
ever changing like the weather

so let this become the season
where your new life can begin

I know
sometimes my memory
can paint a different picture
but I want to see my life as more
than just the pain I've been through.

Whatever path I chose to walk
or however many times I fell,
there's really only one story
I'd ever want to tell myself.

It's a story I am writing
and can't wait to read the rest of.
It starts with how I lost it
and ends with me becoming—

Love.

You can be who you really are now.

The light that's no longer afraid to be seen.
The song that's no longer afraid to be heard.
The love that's no longer afraid to be felt.

You can be who you really are now.

It's who you've always been
underneath it all.

Too often I'd sacrifice parts of myself to avoid being judged or misunderstood, or to avoid making others uncomfortable. Even parts of myself I loved. Even parts of myself that made me who I was. I hid them and let them wither away in secret chambers of my heart as if waiting for permission just to be myself again.

Well, I'm not waiting anymore
for anyone but me.

If others can't handle my honest truth, then perhaps they don't deserve me.

It took me so long to realize this but I'm learning as I go.

There are billions of us on this earth and not a single one outside of us gets to determine what we're worth.

So shine your light, sing your song, feel your love—
release all shame.

Embrace yourself as you are
and others will feel safe to do the same.

This is it.

This is how loving yourself becomes a service to the world.

I've been alive
all this time

even when
I didn't feel like it

even when
I felt
the ashes of my former selves
scatter in the wind

they were never lost

I've been here
all of this time

even when
I couldn't see it

even when
I lost sight of myself

I was never lost

I've been here

I am here

I will be

For years I held on to the wrong things

wrong people
wrong feelings
wrong memories

I held on with such an
unconscious and unwavering vigor
that I barely noticed
how far down they were dragging me

I'm talking so far down
that I barely remembered
what the light in my heart even looked like

let alone felt like

well
it might have taken forever
to make my way back

but I think I finally understood

what these years in the dark meant
to teach me was

"Only hold on to what holds you"

I let you come
this close to me
because I want
to learn to trust

again

to let go
of all the pain I must

to find in me
the love I lost

at some point in my story
I felt it all fall off the page
but
the closer
that you get to me
and the more that I feel safe

I can feel it all
coming back to me

I can feel it all

I can feel

again

I know my future self
is waiting for me
at the dawn of this long night

when we finally meet
we'll dance together
in the shadow softly cast
by the golden morning light

they'll call me by their name
in a voice I always yearned for
and I'll finally remember
not only why I came here

but why I chose to stay

every path has always led to you
every triumph and mistake
every lesson earned from loving
all the parts of me I had to face

and even in the darkest hours
the ones I felt would never end

there
in the breath between the silence
in the whispers of my longings
in the chambers of my spirit
where no one has ever been

there
you sit and wait for me

ever present
ever growing

my source of light within

What was it that weighed
so heavy on my heart these years?

I could've sworn I brought it with me
like I'd always gotten used to

but somewhere along the way

between then
and now
between there
and here

well
I guess I must've dropped it

there is so much
you will have to let go of
to become
who you are meant to be

even the last leaf
of your most beloved tree
will have to fall, inevitably

only to become
part of the soil

from which a new forest will grow

Oh, sweet child of light,

I can still see you in there:
flickering in the dark
you think is your heart—
but it's only the box
you've put yourself in.

You might feel like you're fading,
but I see you.
I see you.

Your art was never something you made—
it's always been who you are.

You've written yourself
out of worse traps than this,
and the key
is always
in the story you tell yourself.

So step out of that box,
my dear.

The world deserves to read you,
see you,
hear you,
feel you.

It deserves your honesty
as much as you do.

There is so much healing in that—
and it all begins with you.

The love you are
is the love you've always been.

And I see you.

I see you.

all this time you were
patiently waiting

for me
to come back
home to myself

oh
so this is what it's like
to be loved
by you

I couldn't find the perfect words
no matter how I tried
so I let my body speak to me
in a language only I know

see
I learn the most
about myself
every time that I
surrender

but my growth
feels less like
"oh, I've learned"
and more like
"I remember"

who I am
has always been
in me

even when I couldn't see it

and the more
I ran from my own pain

the more I had to feel it

facing my truth
meant facing me
and all of my shortcomings

but also giving myself grace
as I began to find my place

and remember what it feels like
to love who I'm becoming

I had forgotten
what it felt like

to let myself
simply be

without the questions
or the worries

without the doubts
or second-guesses

I'd forgotten
even in the storm

I can simply
be

for every storm
will pass
eventually

leaving the soil moist
in its name

and the same clouds
that brought me
thunder

gifted me
this gentle rain

The longer I held on
to my resentment,
the heavier it became.

How many times before
have I hurt myself
in someone else's name?

No one ever forced
this feeling on me
but I convinced myself
they did.

I found a scapegoat
for my sadness
but then I forgot how to live

a life of my own choosing,
as if I never had a choice.

Yet buried underneath
those stories,

I heard a familiar voice:

"You are not trapped
in this.

You are free
to let this go.

The first step
to choosing
your own life

is
learning
to say

no."

I wish
I'd listened
to my body

my stomach knew
before my brain

it pleaded

"all this shame
and self-betrayal
will make me sick
one day"

looking back
I can't remember
if I stayed
for hope or fear

but the pain
fogging my memory
is beginning to clear

with every day
I spend in silence
and return slowly to myself

I can
hold
accept
and let go

of everything I felt

I'm not the victim
of my story

no
I never was

I am someone who learned a lesson
through hardship and loss

it was my own
recurring pattern
I finally had to face

to learn to trust
my truth so deeply
no one could ever
take its place

and in the end
that's what it's all for
I mean
why else go through
all this hell?

every test I've ever overcome
has brought me closer to myself

to this one morning
this one moment
this one feeling
this one breath

cuerpito mío
ya lo logramos

ya finalmente
te escuché

as long as I have myself
I will never be alone

as long as I am honest with myself
there will always be someone who understands me

as long as I see myself as I really am
I won't have to fear being misunderstood

as long as I can trust myself
all my truths will be held sacred

as long as I can hold myself
I will always have the love I deserve

for the longest time
I lost sight
of parts of myself
I used to love
but to my relief
the fog inside my chest
that covered my heartscape
is finally beginning to
clear up

like subtle hints
my soul had left for me
I found traces
of who I used to be
and suddenly
all the love I'd withheld
came rushing back
with the rising sea

I didn't know that
being alone was the easy part

sure
it can be isolating

but I learned
that everything missing in my loneliness
becomes fulfilled in my aloneness

that it's a gift
to get to sit with my own energy
and understand my own complexity

to live my own life being
only who I choose to be

with no one else to use
as an excuse

"it's all because of you"
I've heard myself say a hundred times

but
that's not really choosing then
is it?

if who I am is so fickle
that whoever gets close enough
can rewrite it

then what have I been doing?

being alone really was the easy part

I had no one to test me
push me
or invite me to grow

sure
I had myself
and my lifetime of lessons
to unpack, dissect, embrace

but after that
then what?

It can't all just be me
learning to
love, forgive, and accept
myself.

That is only the first step.

My character's real test
begins the moment
I let others in.

And yes,
I've failed before.

And yes,
I'll fail again.

But each failure
brings me closer
to understanding
my own truth.

Self-love was not waiting for me
hidden in some mountain.

It was in every word I whispered
when I could've screamed as well.

In every time that I chose presence
over my wounded, patterned self.

It was the moment when I finally
unclasped that burning stone

and let myself be seen by others

just as I am

when I'm alone.

There's more than one way of growing.

It doesn't always have to be learning through pain.
Forming through hardship.

That power found in facing your demons
and finding the courage to overcome them.

The warrior's path.

I get it.

I've walked it.

Walked it, stumbled and fallen
a thousand times
down jagged cliffs
only to once again,
broken and battered,
begin to climb—

over and over and every time
higher than ever before.

To the peak of new beginnings,

where farther down the struggler's path
opens into something grander.

Into a path of love
of grace
of forgiveness
of compassion
of understanding
of acceptance
of surrender
of release

of liberation.

Now, we've dragged the weight of ourselves
through the shadows long enough.

I am ready to go further.
I am ready to be lighter.

Come be light with me,
my love.

Come be love with me,
my light.

you still saw light in me
even when I myself could not

I'll always remember that

It's been long enough.

No more dimming our light
or hiding
out of shame
or fear of blinding.

We were always meant to shine
and dance like the flowing tide

in the glow
of the warm and loving
summer sun.

I am listening again
to a voice I'd long forgotten.

In the deepness of my silence
she whispered undying love to me.

How I missed you,
my sweet guiding light.

La voz de mi corazón.

Should I ever lose myself again,
I trust your love will bring me home.

I'm making a promise
to myself
flowing forward
toward the future

as time slows down
but life feels faster

and the sea inside
grows ever vaster

whether the calm or storm
brings despair or hope

I will return to my breath
and let it keep me afloat

I promise myself

Dearest, truest part of me,

I have been watching you closely all of your life. Even before you carried this name. Even before you lived in this body. I have walked by your side through the peaks of your life and along all the bottomless cliffs. I have journeyed with you through valleys of light and held you through all your long nights. I have flown on the wings of your freedom and buried myself in your fear. I have stayed with you through every triumph and heartbreak, every test, every lesson, and together we've sailed across oceans of both calm and despair. I have dreamt all your dreams and continued to believe in you even when you couldn't yourself.

I've seen you through it all—who you've been, who you are, and who you are becoming.

I only want you to remember that the love that guides you, that carries you and walks with you; the love that you share, that you live and breathe—that love, the one that hums beneath all things in its truest, purest essence, has always been the real you. The real me.

You are loved because You Are Love,
and love, we will forever be.

I am standing on the edge of infinity
where all my pasts and futures meet

where everything I've loved and lost
still lives on as a part of me

I'm immersed in this field of forever
weaving dreams from threads of light

and in the depths
of all their frequencies
I can hear a voice reminding me

"the love that you become
will be the love you choose to write"

Have I always been like this?
I wonder,

as I scour through photos and writings
laid out on the floor
like a withered treasure map

of all my failures and triumphs,
my hardships and lessons—

all the stories I've kept alive
to tie my past to my present.

They seem to uncover a pattern,
or a ritual of sorts,

where I start off enamored
but always end up in remorse.

Does my longing for freedom
outweigh my need for connection?

Is it fear of the other
or love for myself
that leads me
to seek liberation?

Have I always been like this?

Growing up, I felt
small and afraid—

that unless I had someone
to hold on to,
I would never be safe.

All the movies and books,
they all told me the same.

So I did what I knew:
held on as hard
as I possibly could.

But soon enough
my holding turned into grasping
and my grasping turned into crushing.

The unbearable weight of attachment
in the hand of an unhealed child
only ever made me feel smaller.

I'd tell myself,
"This is who I am, I suppose.
This is all I know.
This is all I can be."

Until decades later,
when my true character was tested—

and in a moment of crisis,
a crossroad of lifelines,

I finally learned to say no.

I finally dared to choose me.

To remain strong when being pummeled
under overwhelming pressure

and to allow myself fluidity
for when life suddenly changes.

Both things
the same river taught me.

I'm slowly picking myself back up.

Not at the pace I'd necessarily want
but at the pace that my body needs right now.

With patience and grace.
Love and compassion.

I know I can figure it out.

I already know what works best for me.

Whenever I resist, control, or try to force things,
it inevitably leads to frustration and exhaustion.

Whenever I let go, trust, and surrender,
life has a way of bringing me exactly where I need to be.

For me it's both about having an intention
and then surrendering to trust.

I have to keep reminding myself of this time and time again
to avoid falling into patterns that do nothing but hurt me.

That is what this is,

just a gentle reminder.

bask in the sun
dance in the rain
forgive yourself
reclaim your name
let the past go
clear your mind
be new again

while we still have time

we
still
have
time

I am no longer
trying
to make life happen

I am
simply
letting it
be

to carve and pour
its way
out through
the deepest secret
parts of me

I hid away
starved
and swore

my light
would never shine

again

and yet

the night
I chose
myself

my silence
finally
sang

again

you fell upon my withered garden
like a soft nurturing rain

and this longing soil
once dry and barren

sprang back to life again

love will never ask you
to be less of what you are

I am
trusting

that
everything
is aligning

in the best
possible way

so that both
my spirit
and my body

can be held
through it all

I thought it would last forever
but the storm finally passed

and in its place
all that remained

was a calm, forgiving rain

every time I dare say no
I get to safekeep my own energy

every time I let things go
I create space for what is meant for me

every time I accept help
a broken part of me recovers

every time I choose myself
I create more love I can gift to others

I never felt like I belonged
anywhere at all
until I carved a place out for myself
deep in my aloneness
and breathed the words I longed to feel

my skin
my tears
my hair
my fears
my love
my bones
my words

are home

The season
of settling for less
than what I give
and I deserve

is over.

From this moment forward
the only people allowed to share
sacred space in my life

are those who embody selfless love
and reciprocate my energy.

Who want to build upon my life
and be mutual pillars of support.

Who fan the flames inside my heart
and yearn to see me thrive.

Who celebrate my triumphs
and hold me in my failures.

Who see past my shortcomings
and believe in my potential.

Who allow me to be human,
with all my virtues and my flaws,

and still choose to love me through it all.

I am done using the past
as an excuse not to be better.

Life is only moving forward
and so will I.

So am I.

I've come to understand

that the recurring stories
in my life are not meant
to torment me
and make me feel smaller

I've been given a chance
time after time
again and again
to learn to trust
and hold myself
across vast oceans of
projections and interpretations

this lesson is mine
regardless of who
or what
or why

the characters and setting
might change
but the lesson remains

each time deeper
and more challenging
than the last

like a teacher
once told me

"if you pray for courage,
you will be tested"

well
I prayed to finally
be myself again

and so
this new retelling of old stories
is another invitation
to face all the versions that exist
within me and in others

to shed the layers of shadows
that made their home in my body

and to finally be able
to stand in the truth
of who I choose to be

in the strength of my courage
in the softness of my sadness
in the honesty of my anger
in the joy of my belonging
in the peace of my presence
in the safety of my intimacy

in the trust of my own story

Who you used to be
does not determine who you can become.

Nothing's written in stepping stones.

I am standing on the crossing
where all my past and futures meet

who I was
who I am
and who I'm meant to be

The garden we tended together
had long since overgrown.
One day,
in my silent longing,
I went back and dug it up.
To my surprise,
I found a certain sense of serenity
buried underneath that lush forgotten memory.
There was an unspoken beauty in that abandon—
in that letting go.
I couldn't understand it back then,
or perhaps I didn't want to.
Now,
the deeper I go,
the more your words resound in me.

I had to tend to my own garden if I ever wanted to grow.

I got so caught up in the stories
I told myself about you
that I didn't even stop to notice
how you were hurting too.

You were hurting too.

I took too long to understand
but Time has a way
of prying things open.

I mean eyes,
I mean hearts,
I mean hands.

So whatever I was holding on to,
whichever You I thought I knew,

it's all gone now.

It took me a while but now I see it.
How hard it must have been for you.

Seeing myself now, though,
having come this far
and still shining through,
it all seems so clear.

What you left me,
that day you disappeared . . .

really was a gift.

I go in and out of it
constantly these days

the ebb and flow between
clarity and confusion
hope and despair
relief and agony

acceptance
and resentment

there are moments
where everything feels
aligned
and I trust
that the worst is over
but

then the tide suddenly shifts
again

and I unwillingly
get carried away
with it

unlearning
can be a lot harder
than learning
and
it takes courage
to still float unafraid
after nearly drowning

I can see
how all the patterns
that were once
written in sand
over time
ended up
becoming
carvings

engraved on my stone body

an abandoned terrain

a reminder of all the places in me
where I still carry this pain

but now that I see it

well

nothing's the same

"written in stone"
doesn't mean
I can't change

confusion for clarity
despair for hope
agony for relief

or resentment
for acceptance

as hard as it's been
I feel I can finally say . . .

Let the swelling tide
come rushing in

I'm no longer afraid
of being swept away

I was in a silent dream:

walking barefoot through a moonlit forest,
mossy soil between my toes,
when I came upon a creature with silver glowing fur.

Was it a rabbit, fox, or wolf?

I couldn't really tell.

I hadn't seen you in so long,
I didn't know how you wore your hair anymore.

Your quiet gaze,
undecipherable as ever

and yet I understood.

"I know I cannot change
the resentment in your heart,
but at the very least,
I can choose
how you live on
in mine."

I let out the world's longest sigh,

so deep,
so freeing
that it almost woke me,

and you
just scurried off

without ruffling a single leaf,
without once stopping to look back at me

—*closure.*

Sometimes I am happiest alone.
Sometimes I need to feel supported.

Sometimes I feel confident, strong, and centered,
and other times I feel insecure, scared, and unbalanced.

Sometimes I catch glimpses of my highest self
and then I struggle to recognize the work I've done.

Sometimes I understand completely.
Sometimes I am completely lost.

It's taken a lifetime of "sometimes" to understand
the ebb and flow at which my heart grows.

To feel I am finally in a place
where I can honor and embrace it.

To love and become the complete version of me
I've been dreaming of all my life.

I realize now that my spirit needs both
to dance in darkness and to bask in light.

I'm doing the best I can
with what I have.

It might not be perfect
but at least it's mine.

It's gotten harder over time,

transmuting these frustrations
into an honest expression.

I keep reminding myself:

As long as it is true to me,
as long as I'm true to myself,

that's all that really matters, right?

As long as it is true to me . . .

I can be satisfied.

If today it feels harder
to love yourself,
then at least try
to be compassionate:

"I know in my heart
I am trying the best that I can."

If you find
that you can't feel compassionate,
then at least try to be patient:

"I know that healing
is never a straight line
and changing the patterns
I've repeated for so long
is going to take time."

If even patience escapes you,
then at the very least be honest
and simply observe
whatever comes out:

"Today was hard for me
and tomorrow who knows,
but at least I am able to see it for now."

If anything,
know
none of it is in vain:

"If yesterday I suffered
for ten hours straight
and today it lasted just two minutes less,
it might seem like it's nothing,
but I know I am on it—

the path back to love
is being carved in my name."

Wherever you focus your intention,
there your love will grow.

Last night
I walked my hands over every part
of my aging landscape

every mound and every hill
every valley and every canyon
every cliff and every fault line
every quiet landslide

and with my tender touch
I asked for her forgiveness

for ever feeling shame
for not taking better care
for letting myself crumble
under the weight of all these years

and all the while
she still

always held me
always carried me
always persevered

it took
a thousand droughts
and fires
for me to finally see

my body is the Earth
and she is me

Let me stay here
for a moment
in this fleeting calm
after the storm
where the light I knew
still lived in me
pierced through
just to remind me

I am here
I am with you

alone together
together alone

nothing belongs to us

nothing
but this moment

it is ours
just for an instant

and then it will float away

I'll float away

let this moment be
whatever it needs to be

the more I surrender to this moment
the more I embrace instead of resist
the more I let go instead of hold on

the more my life opens its heart to me

I stopped searching
for forever
in the hearts of others
and found
Presence
in the fleeting wind.

life looks a lot different than it used to
but it feels closer to my dreams

a quiet morning
surrounded by nature

as simple as
time together

in peace

I never needed
to do more.

I have always
been enough.

The less I do,
the more I am,

and the more I have
to give to you.

For the longest time I mourned
that the person I loved being
would never return to me

so
imagine my surprise
when the night I let them go

I got to fall in love again
with a new version of me

My mind dredged up
an old familiar storm the other day.

My first reaction was expressing it
but I know hurtful words can only leave
a wreck in their wake.

Afterward, I tried repressing it
but there is only so much
a levee can take before it breaks.

Then at last I sat observing it,
without judgment, shame, or blame,
and in an instant she passed right through me.

I could see her hidden beauty.

What she had brought me
and what she'd taught me
were meant to shake me
so it could wake me.

I found the truth in what I was feeling
and in my heart there was no doubt.

All these storms served to remind me:

If it's coming up,
it's coming out.

the day I traded
my resentment
for gratitude

my whole life changed

Being able to give thanks for my hardships does not invalidate my past experience. It's not bypassing or repressing. It's not celebrating, justifying, or condoning past abuse, abandon, betrayal, violence, or trauma. It is saying I survived and I am taking ownership of my life instead of being a victim of it.

I'm not thankful I was hurt.

I am thankful because on the other side of that pain was a whole new life waiting for me, filled with new people, places, experiences, and lessons that I would have never known otherwise.

Saying thanks for my hardships puts my power back in my hands and rewrites how my mind relates to my suffering, shifting from

"It's the reason I am the way I am"

to

"It's the storm that fanned
the flame in my heart
and gave way
to my biggest transformation."

I made the choice
to live again
and every step
I've taken
upon this earth
since then
has become holy

It was a stormy day.
I've had a lot of those lately.

I wanted to stay in, of course. To stay in that false sense of safety my fear and shame give me, just because they've been with me for so long. But, thankfully, I didn't.

I went out.

Partly forced.
Partly brave.
Out into the gray.

And to my surprise, after weathering the storm (or more like letting it pass), all the colors I'd kept hidden in my fractured heart of glass through sea and clouds they burst through to paint the world in every shade of love I knew.

The love I knew.

I knew it was still in me somewhere.

a dormant flame
reawakens within me

like a long-forgotten ceremony

see,
these embers carry memory

and returning
is remembering

el fuego en mi corazón

all this time

I didn’t know
you were this close to me

but
it was always you
wasn’t it?

filling up my lungs
and beating in my chest

you were always here

in me

Nurturing self-love can be challenging since it asks us to overcome feelings no one ever taught us how to face. Be patient with yourself. It's okay to not be there just yet. It's okay to feel loneliness. It's okay to need others. Just try and remember, even if there is no one else . . .

There's still you.

I know that might not feel like enough sometimes but small acts of love over time can create huge transformations.

Try this:

Hold yourself in your arms for a second, if you need it, and repeat to yourself in your most nurturing voice,

"I am held. Even if only by myself. I am held."

Sit in that feeling for a moment and truly hold yourself.

This is you becoming the love that you yearn for.

“Don’t be afraid to grow,”

she said,

and an entire forest
grew from my chest.

Return to me,
luz de mi corazón.

You have nothing to be afraid of
anymore.

there will suddenly
come a time

once you have surrendered

when seemingly
out of nowhere

but in reality
from everywhere

everything
will
align
again

you just have to let it happen

The same rising tide
that swept me away
from the parts I loved most
in myself
was the one
that eventually would
carry me all the way
back home

to me.

Now
every time I touch the water,
I remember.

If I hadn't learned surrender,

I would still be lost at sea.

I am a multidimensional being.

I nurture, accept, and give love to all parts of me: my light, my shadow, and every shade of gray in between. I bring out whichever one is needed and honor it as neither less or more but as an essential part of my most authentic self. I do not limit myself to others' interpretations or projections. I do not limit my capacity to surprise even myself. I am vast and I am limitless. I am expansive and ever changing.

I am a multidimensional being.

I understand you better now,
my light.

You have been guiding me home
from the start.

I just had to learn
to see you,

not just with my eyes
but with my heart.

The time and place
you're meant to be
is no other
than here and now.

The heart gate opening.

All the way to the ends of the earth
I've walked the invisible path
only to find you
to be with you
to become you
to love you

my deepest
truest
self

There's a voice tucked away
in the belly of your silence,
whispering your longings
to the river and the woods.

If you surrender
and trust it,
fearless,
faithful,
it will guide you—

down the stream,
through the mountain,
past the valley,

back to you.

I waited,
just like you asked me,
for as long as I possibly could
just to hear a whisper of yours
in the wind,
but your silence
meant it was over.
For good.
I thought long and hard
about what that even meant.
If it's over, what do I have left?

"Oh,
mi alma,
mi mundo,
my love,
my breath,

you still have
a whole universe
tucked away
in your chest."

I found her,
not lost
but wandering
in my haziest of memories.

I hardly remember my dreams
but I remember what she told me.

"I was holding back on living
and then life went on without me."

I caught myself,
not lost
but wandering
in my frailest of boundaries.

My deepest wounds.
My patterns.

My self-fulfilling prophecy.

See,

I've been hiding from my fear,
from my guilt and my shame,
but no matter how this pain rhymes,
I know it's not the same.

Neither am I.

I just need to remember,
in every single breath.

Deep inhale—
"I am more than who I was."

Long exhale, with a sigh—
"I am coming out of hiding.
I won't let life pass me by."

You can have it back

this sea of shame
never belonged to me

I can't believe for how long
I let shallow waters get to me

I was drowning on the surface
when I knew the truth
lay in the depths

how could I ever see
the love surrounding me
with my face buried in my chest?

so I made myself a promise
and whispered it
into the sea

I said . . .

there is no one on this earth
who knows my truth better than me

all the work that I have done
the darkness I've overcome

all the years of facing myself
until I'd finally become
someone worthy of
my own self-love
my compassion
my forgiveness

the stories that shaped my heart
in ways no one ever got to witness

so whom do I owe for
who I am now?

who gets to see who I can be?

only the ones that reflect back my love

and all the rest?

well . . .

you can have them back

their sea of shame never belonged to me

Remember all of those times
you felt like giving up?
Like you weren't strong enough?
Like the suffering would never end
and you were powerless to change anything?

Yeah, I remember them too.

And yet
here we are,

still breathing,
still healing,
still learning,
still loving.

All these tests we have faced
were never meant to break us.

They were meant to shape us.

So then,
somewhere in all of that,
we can find space for gratitude
for these lessons that have made us.

I have to say,
from where I am standing,
looking at all of us still growing,

I deeply believe in who we are becoming

and I'm thankful we're still here.

I'm so thankful I'm still here.

there is nothing outside of me
keeping me from living a life I can love

there never really was

I can see that now

The parts of me that once used to be
always pushing, pulling, or holding back
have now become the ones that live
for giving, receiving, and opening up.

Nothing outside of me had to change
for everything in my life to.

Years have passed
and here I am now,
in the same place I used to be,
yet everything feels new to me.

Nothing outside of me had to change.

Just the stories I would tell myself back then.

The best thing I ever did for my heart
was allow myself
to begin again.

All those years I spent in darkness
served their purpose
but I'm ready now
to come out to the light.

All that weight I used to carry
served its purpose
but I'm ready now
to finally become light.

I choose.
I allow.
I accept.
I become.

Light and lightness.
Lightness and light.

Come,
be light with me.

You've been crawling
in that crippling self-doubt
for way too long.

Almost as if you've forgotten
how the crashing ocean carved
the very ground you stand upon.

But you,
my love,

you are.

You are the waves that shape the earth
and you are the earth forever changing.

You are light
and you are shadow,
for eternity embracing.

All that crawling brought you here,
to this moment—
your golden hour.

Time to stand back up again,
my dear.

Time to step into your power.

I had it all wrong

it was never about going back
to a better time
or a better 'who you used to be'

it was about starting again
again
and again
a thousand times if you need to

however many times it takes
to shed all the versions of you
who had to die and become soil
for you to grow
for you to see
for you to remember
for you to finally come home

to me
to you
to us
to Love

This heart I offer you
is the most precious gift I have

it was forged in the sun
and cured in the sea

it faced storms and loss
death and rebirth
more times than I can count

until finally—
once it was so broken
that it cracked itself wide open—
from its depths
flowed an ocean
of only unconditional love

that's when I understood
what I was really made of

I was never meant to only be
a storm in someone else's sea

I was meant to grow
with the ebb and flow
of this boundless Sea of Light in me

to learn to hold without grasping
to witness without claiming

to return to me what I thought was lost
and feel its warm glow in my hand

this heart I offered myself
is the greatest gift I have

I knew you had it in you.

Even after all this time
and everything you've gone through.

Still,
you kept on growing,
past the roots of all your suffering.

You faced
your truth
and learned
to love yourself
not in spite of
but because of it.

These hardships
could've broken you
but instead

look at you now.

Standing stronger than ever.
More present than ever.
More grateful than ever before.

Just look at you now,
mi corazón.

I knew.

I knew you had it in you.

all I've been
all I've loved
all I've lost

I honor and release
back into the source

back into
the fountain of love
where all things are transformed

I am ready to let go now
I am ready to begin again

I am

I am

I am

epilogue : evening star

The album *Inscape* by Alexandra Stréliski plays in the background.

It's Thursday, my favorite day of the week.

Fifty years ago, my daughter was born on a Thursday, and it's always been a special day for me. It's ceremoniously our family day. A tradition we passed down to her children as well, and then my grandkids made it their own.

My oldest grandchild, whom I've always had a deep connection with, is always the first to arrive and the last to leave. "Hey, Papapa, can we look over your books again?" he asks.

My memory is an album full of stories and photographs of all the love I ever lived. It took me a long time, but in my late thirties I finally put it all together into a first book, which later became a series.

It made remembering and retelling my stories so much easier.

"Here it is," he says, as he takes a seat next to the bed I've been lying in for days. He opens the book to the first chapters, and there's me: young and strong; my hair, all wet from bathing in the river, hanging down to my shoulders. The sun setting over the mountains. The silence and depth of my aloneness. The birth of my art.

We go over every poem and photo, and the stories behind them. I recall how I learned to love myself in those mountains and how I took that self-love with me to travel across the world.

He leafs through the pages and stops at one of his favorite ones: a photo of me at a crossroads in life. It was what we called back in the day a "mirror selfie," where I'm holding a Sage's Staff in one hand and a Hobby Horse in the other. "That was a pivotal moment for me," I say, in a deep and warm voice. "Back then, I was always scared that I would have to choose between being a traveling sage or a family man."

"And look at you now, Papapa! Look at the life you built. Look at the dreams you brought to life. Who would've thought? Not even you could imagine what adventures life still had in store for you. All you had to do was follow your truth."

My eyes water at the thought. This kid always knows what to say to me to get me emotional. He passes over some pages and lands on a photo of me with my teenage daughter on a remote mountaintop in one of our yearly father-daughter trips. The kind of thing I thought I'd never get to do turned out to be our favorite thing to do together.

If I had given in to my fear of feeling trapped, moments like this would have never existed.

I think back to those first three years when my daughter was born and realize they were probably the most important years of my life.

For a long time, I carried resentment in my heart—toward her mother, toward people who hurt me, toward circumstances that I let victimize me. It's crazy to think that that resentment was the key to everything changing in my life. By that I mean, letting go of that resentment was the key to changing my entire life.

"You needed to make space," he says. "Resentment was holding you back from seeing how truly blessed you were. How supported you were. How seen and cherished you were. Letting go of resentment was your path toward truth and liberation."

"Damn, kid, how'd you get so wise?" I ask while laughing.

"I've been listening to your stories for over eighteen years, Papapa. I've learned from you. Learned from your mistakes, but most of all, learned from your love. Few people ever get to live a life as full as yours. You're proof that things can change. That we can live our dreams. That our hardships were never meant to break us, but shape us. That we can transmute our suffering into bliss and satisfaction. You proved it to yourself, and you paved a way for our lineage. This love you left us will live through me and in generations to come. I'm so proud to be your grandson. I'm so proud of you."

I smile with every fiber of my body
and close my eyes one last time . . .

I am so satisfied.

Acknowledgments

Fifteen years ago, an astrologer told me I was going to write a book someday. I shrugged it off in disbelief and kept on with my life. "I'm an artist, not a writer," I told myself. Well, after a few life-changing catastrophes, a solo trip around the world, a marriage, a child, a chronic illness, and a divorce, here we are. I should probably go find him again and give him a copy.

This book wouldn't exist without the energy, love, and support of countless people over the last seven years. First, I want to thank my book agent, Steven Harris, for your guidance, expertise, and always-caring heart. You helped keep me afloat and accountable through one of the most challenging seasons of my life. I will forever be grateful that you helped me land my dream book deal.

To my editor, Michelle Herrera, thank you for not only diving into this journey with me, but for helping this book become something much grander than I ever could've imagined. Your sensitivity, openness, and heartfelt questions unlocked parts of my heart that deserved to be in these pages. Thank you for seeing me.

To the entire team at Primero Sueño, thank you for being such a lovely, patient, and generous group of people to work with. From the art to the book design, thank you for bringing my vision to life and elevating it.

To my dear friend and mentor, Kym Pham, whose writing containers quite literally saved me at one of the lowest points of my life, thank you. You always saw the light in me when even I couldn't and helped me remember that I was always a writer.

To the mother of my child, Christine, thank you for giving me the greatest gift of my life, our Mar de Luz, and for believing in my potential in a way that became the catalyst for all of this. I'm grateful for, and proud of, our coparenting journey.

To my writer friends who inspired me to believe in myself, Diego Perez, Brianna Pastor, and Ron Lim, thank you for paving the way for me and countless others. You're living proof of what's possible when you commit yourself to your craft in service of others. Thank you for being a guiding light in the dark.

To my parents, Irma and Juan, thank you for trusting that your weird, sensitive, "alternative" kid would someday figure himself out. Thank you for letting me be who I've always been and for being the wind in my sails.

To everyone I've ever loved, those who've stayed and those who've gone, especially the ones who held me through this most challenging season of my life, I wouldn't have made it through the storm without you.

Lastly, I want to thank two people who helped shape my heart, my writing, and my sense of purpose and who aren't with us anymore, Janine and Benson. My memories of you are endless golden fields of light. You are forever a part of my heart, and my love for you will always live on in these words.

Thank you. Thank you. Thank you.

fernando samalot is a poet, photographer, and audiovisual artist from Puerto Rico.

His writing and artistic practice explores themes such as the relationship between light and darkness, duality, unconditional love, loss, vulnerability, connection, surrender, and presence—allowing space to honor all the different aspects that shape us into multidimensional beings.

A passionate believer in the healing power of art, he shares his inner world in hopes of creating connection and inviting the viewer to tap into something deeper in themselves.

A sacred place inside us
where our love is safe to grow.

You can follow his writing and art journey on all socials at @fernandosamalot.